COTHAM

ARLEY HILL & CHELTENHAM RD. 236.

1. Arley Chapel named after its benefactor John Holmes, who was born in Arley, Worcestershire. The foundation stone laid by Richard Ash in 1845. It was built in an Italian style, and today, it is a Polish Catholic Church.

2. Arley Hill known as Lamp Black Hill in the 1850's. It was the main thoroughfare from Cotham and Redland to Durdham Downs. This unusual snow scene taken by EC Stevens who lived at 12 Arley Hill.

3. This early car outside Arley Chapel, c.1914-18, the headlamps shaded. The driver W.S. Shepherd a butcher. The car registration No. AE 6781, a Bristol number.

4. A festive occasion at Arley Chapel Soldiers Institute, in 1911. Attractively laid tables awaiting soldiers to enjoy a Christmas dinner.

COTHAM

5. This view of Cheltenham Road is included as it shows the Railway Bridge of the Temple Mead's - Severn Beach line that runs through Cotham and Redland. The next station to the right is Redland.

6. Looking in the same direction the road in flood. Tram No. 119 en route for Durdham Downs via Zetland Road. The floodwaters created mainly when the Cran Brook overflowed in heavy rain.

COTHAM

7. Sydenham Road built in the 1840's. This view at the steep part as it joins Nugent Hill. It then continues and joins with Cotham Brow.

8. Eastfield Road situated near the bottom of Cotham Brow. At the far end of the road, the embankment of Temple Meads-Severn Beach railway. The postcard postally used in 1909.

9. A view of the houses and gardens on the left hand side going down Cotham Brow. Large semi-detached house with decorative gateposts and front walls, a feature of Victorian Cotham.

10. St Matthews Road from Clevedon Terrace. St. Matthews Church at the far end of the road. Bishop Ryder consecrated the Church in April 1835. It's peel of eight bells presented by John Bagley.

COTHAM

11. Victoria Walk built c.1840, and in the foreground, Freemantle Square. These three storey houses facing a small green. Published by Brightman of Redland, and posted in 1907.

12. Bristol Youth Hostel on the corner of St Matthews Road. No longer a Youth Hostel, (now situated in Broad Quay.)

COTHAM

13. Cotham Road built in c.1829. This view from Cotham Road South, looking in the direction of the Homeopathic Hospital. The postcard sent from Freemantle Place, Cotham in 1907.

14. A garden fete held at "Lyndale", Cotham Road, quite an occasion with ladies in stylish dresses and large hats. Probably a fund raising occasion, a man giving an address. The man to his left appears to be asleep!

15. Western College situated on the right hand corner at the top of Cotham Road. This College used for the education of young men proposing to become Congregational ministers. This multi view shows all the main rooms of the college.

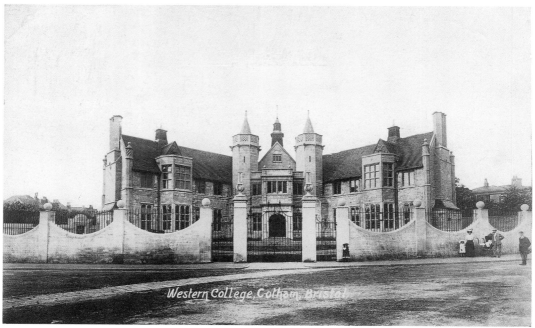

16. Western College showing its distinctive frontage. It was founded by the Independents, which was established at Plymouth in c.1846. The college was opened on October 7th 1901, with further improvements in 1905.

17. The Principals house built adjoining the college.

18. The hall and stairway within the College, wood panelling around the walls and stairs. The door complimenting the plain walls.

BRISTOL HOMŒOPATHIC HOSPITAL, FROM THE AIR

19. An ariel view of the Homeopathic Hospital and the surrounding district. The large building above centre, the hospital, and immediately behind Western College. The church on the right Highbury Chapel, and the long road in the centre, Tyndall's Park Road.

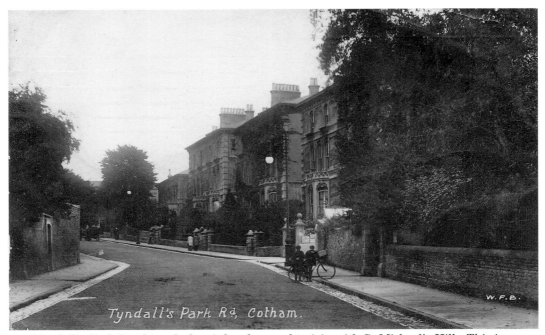

Tyndall's Park Rd, Cotham.

20. Tyndall's Park Road just before it bends round to join with St Michael's Hill. This in more leisurely days, two delivery boys, stopping for a chat! Postcard postally used in 1907.

21. The Prince of Wales laying the foundation stone of the Homeopathic Hospital, on his visit to Bristol on the 10th June 1921.

22. The imposing frontage and front porch of the Homeopathic Hospital facing Cotham Road. The hospital was built and equipped by W. Melville Wills, President, in memory of his son Captain Bruce Melville-Wills, who lost his life during the 1914-18 war.

23. The back view of the hospital showing the lily pond and flower gardens.

24. Highbury Chapel from St Michael's Hill. It was opened for worship in 1843, and designed by William Butterfield. (1814-1900). The first pastor was the Rev. David Thomas.

25. St Joseph's Convent in Cotham Hill, built between late 1860-1870's for the Little Sisters of the poor, and designed by Charles Hansom. A home for men and women.

26. The Laundry room of St Joseph's, sinks, mangle and laundry baskets, and the inevitable wet floor!

27. Cotham Hill with many shops, their sunblinds down. This postcard postally used in 1905. In the distance the tower of Tyndall Baptist Church built c. 1868.

28. Cotham Hill at the Whiteladies Road end. Shops include a hat shop and fish supplier. Into the main road, a cab stand, and far right the end wall of the Imperial Hotel.

29. Morley's Library and Stationers at No. 50, Cotham Hill. Many stationers had small libraries where customers could borrow books. This view c. 1912, their delivery cycle parked on the curb.

30. An early view of Cotham Hill c. 1905. The premises of Crocker Refreshments Bar, at No. 33. Also called The Whiteladies Tavern. To the left builder, Henry Cook, and on the other side of the restaurant a small newsagent.

A Bit of Cotham Hill.

Cotham Grove and Lovers Walk

August 20th /04. Bristol

95869

31. This view from Cotham Grove, where it joins with Redland Grove, the trees lined Lovers Walk adjoining Cotham Gardens. Redland Grove crosses the road over the railway line, and continues to join with Redland Road.

32. Looking in the same direction as picture 31. The snow gives a different aspect. This view from Freemantle Road, with Cotham Grove on the left. The street lamp in the middle of the junction.

33. The grounds for Cotham Gardens given to Bristol Corporation by the Fry family in 1879. The park opened in 1881, and consisted of several winding pathways, many trees incorporated within the area, with a bandstand. The roof of Redland Station can be seen to the left of the bandstand.

34. Lovers Walk, the tree lined pathway-adjoining Cotham Gardens, included with the garden as a public open space. This steep aspect looking toward Cotham. Postcard postally used in 1912.

COTHAM - REDLAND

35. This post-war view of Redland Station, with a view of the waiting room on the Cotham side. The station opened in 1897.

36. A c. 1920 view of a corner of Cotham Gardens, children posing for the photographer. Between the trees a house in Redland Road.

37. An earlier view, on a very wet day the line flooded between the line. Advertisements on the waiting room wall, and old lamps. In the distance on the left Redland signal box.

38. Redland signal box the up and down line in the foreground, and a glimpse of houses in Redland Road.

39. Cotham Gardens in the snow, looking towards the station, and Redland beyond.

40. Another snow scene from Redland Court, showing the decorative pillars of the gateway and beyond Lovers Walk originally the carriageway to Redland Court.

41. Lovers Walk where the path levels out giving a glimpse of Redland Court between the line of trees. A tram en route for Zetland Road, and the Tramway Centre c. 1910.

42. The tram No. 135, on the Durham Downs, Zetland Road route. The tram turns left here into South Road. This view c. 1938.

43. Redland Court built from a design by John Straham, and was completed in 1735, for John Cossins, a grocer from London. The house became Redland High School in 1883. This postcard posted in 1913.

44. Lovers Walk as it approaches the bridge over the railway line. George Edwards of Redland Court gave the Redland part of Lovers Walk (beyond the railway bridge) as a permanent open space for the citizens of Bristol in 1884.

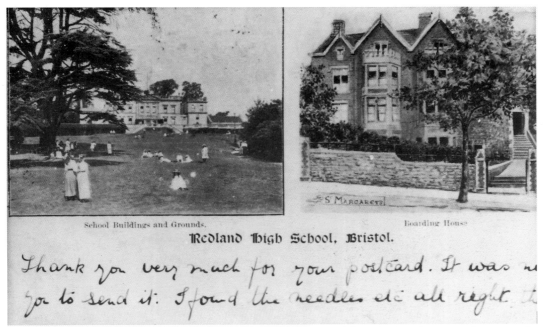

School Buildings and Grounds.   Boarding House

Redland High School, Bristol.

Thank you very much for your postcard. It was n̲
you to send it. I found the needles etc all right t̲

45. This multi view of Redland High School c. 1905 shows girls enjoying the extensive grounds in the front of the school. The boarding house used by staff and pupils.

46. St. Ronans Avenue from Ravenswood Road.   The double bay villas, is typical of the architecture of the area. This view c. 1910, with Waverley Road connecting at the far end.

Zetland Road, Redland, Bristol.   No. 533.   5. 9. 1904.   J.S.L.

47. Zetland Road from the corner of Lower Redland Road c. 1904. This early view shows a tram and cart further down the road, in the direction of Cheltenham and Gloucester Road.

C. Stevens.   W. R. ROGERS, LANDSCAPE GARDENER, AND FLORIST,
ZETLAND ROAD.

48. Mr. W. R. Rogers, landscape gardener and florist in Zetland Road. The Greenhouse shop adjoining the house c. 1908. the railway Embankment of the Temple Meads-Severn Beach line behind the house.

49. The proposed plan of Trinity Presbyterian Church in Cranbrook Road, on the corner with Kersteman Road.

50. The constructors for the building of the church, the Bristol firm of William Cowlin & Son. This view from Elton Road shows the church with scaffolding around the tower.

51. Trinity Church, Cranbrook Road, opened for services October 2nd 1901, and was conducted by the Rev. Dr. J. Thain Davidson. Up till then only the lecture hall and classrooms had been built.

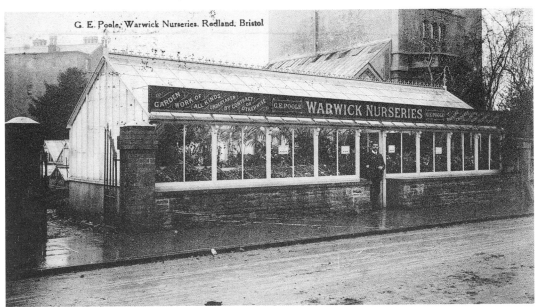

52. Warwick Garden Nurseries, in Warwick Road, owned by Mr. G.E. Poole, c. 1907. The postcard sent by Mr. Poole confirming that he had received a valued order from Mr. Tedder of Westbury-on-Trym.

53. Redland Park Church in Redland Park. The original church on this site opened in September 4th 1861. It was destroyed in the last war, on December 2nd 1940. The new church built; and consecrated on June 1st 1957.

54. A family group standing at the front entrance of their house, "Fernleigh", in Northumberland Road. This road connects with Zetland Road and Carnarvon Road.

55. Chandos Road a rather narrow thoroughfare off of Hampton Road, with a good selection of shops. The car no. AE 8797, being admired by passers by.

56. St. Saviour's Church, Woolcott Park, formerly an iron church removed from Tyndall's Park in 1875. This present church consecrated by the Bishop of Bristol on May 30th 1882. Next door to the church, E. F. Jones builders, with many advertisements on the walls, conveying his range of services.

57. Woodstock Road, an attractive snow scene. It begins from Redland Green, and continues past Redland High School, and then joins with Clarendon Road.

58. Redland Road taken by Brightman, who lived at 61, Redland Road, the small arrow indicates the house.

59. Redland Hill from Lower Redland Road, the trees in the centre distance on Redland Green. The tram en route for Durdham Downs.

60. Redland Green from Redland Hill. Redland Church can be seen at the end of the tree lined road, originally a private chapel, attached to Redland Court.

61. Redland Church, of Georgian period, originally a Chapel built in 1743. John Straham who also designed Redland Court designed the church. The foundation stone laid in 1740.

62. The Bishop's Palace built on part of Redland Green. It was destroyed in an air raid in the last war. The Bishop's residence now in Clifton Hill.

63. Redland Green also known as The Dell. An attractive open space bordered mainly by Cossins Road (after John Cossins former owner of Redland Court), Metford Road and Redland Green Road.

64. A weeklong Naval Carnival held on Redland Green in July tickets 3d. Miss Daisy May, (Principle Girl at the Princes Theatre) appearing in a Concert Party. Also appearing Little Edna Maude (she had recently danced before Royalty).

65. The Police Station in Lower Redland Road, between West and East Shrubbery, built in 1890.

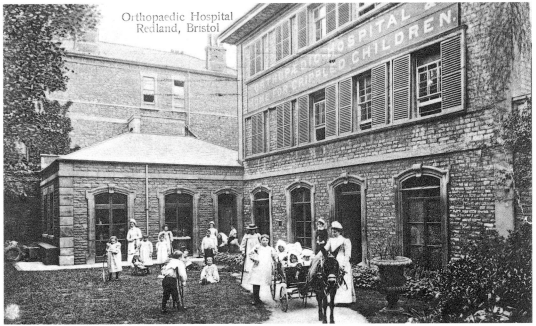

66. The Orthopaedic Hospital and home for crippled children, in Grove Road, near Blackboy Hill. It opened in 1876, for children who needed medical help, combined by education. Postcard posted in 1905.

67. Tram no. 236 at the tram stop at the bottom of Redland Hill c. 1936.

68. Redland College in the centre of this ariel view. Redland Hill in the foreground and curving right Redland Road, and at the top Durdham Downs. Published by Soames of Cardiff.

PART OF MACHINE ROOM.

JAMES TAYLOR HARRIS LTD.
ART PRINTERS, Cliftonville Studios,
Redland, BRISTOL.

69. An interesting view of the machine room of James Taylor Harris Ltd: fine art printers. The Clifton Villa studios situated in Redland. c. 1912.

The Collegiate School, Redland.

70. Redland Bank acquired in 1924, and became Collegiate School, opening in 1929; taking pupils aged 4 years to 19 years. The house situated in Redland Hill. The school moved to Langford Court in 1939, then in 1945 to Winterbourne House, Winterbourne.

71. Queen Victoria Convalescent Home formed Bristol's celebration of the Diamond Jubilee, of Queen Victoria in 1897. A fund was set up, and a plan for the project was assured by a donation from Sir E. P. Wills, of a house called Waynflete (a former boy's school,) with three acres of grounds, which could be adapted for the purpose.

72. The back view of the Convalescent Home. Queen Victoria opened it on November 15th 1899. Further running costs were needed, and donations were received from Sir E. P. Wills, Mr. P. H. Vaughan and Mr. Joseph Storrs-Fry. A "Shilling Fund", sponsored by the Western Daily Press, raised 63,766 shillings from the public.

73. Another view of the Convalescent Home, a close up view at the back, showing the terrace. Convalescents of all ages, with their nurses.

74. An early Motor Bus run by Bristol Tramways and Carriage Co. Ltd. The route Westbury, Henleaze Road, Etloe Road and Redland. c. 1906.

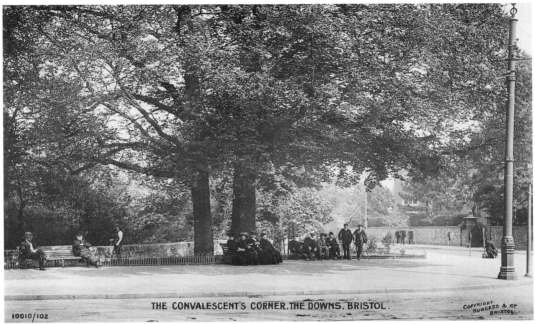

THE CONVALESCENT'S CORNER. THE DOWNS. BRISTOL.

75. The Convalescent corner, patients from the convalescent home relaxing on seats outside The Glen.

Durdham Down, Bristol. 280.

76. A view towards the top of Redland Hill from Durham Downs, a tram just emerging. Small houses and trees on the corner blocking the view of the Convalescents Home.

77. The Glen Pavilion popular for military bands and varied entertainment in the 1920's. The Glen a former quarry.

78. The pathway within The Glen, bordered by wooden fencing, two boy stewards in smart uniform. The auditorium just visible through the trees.

79. One of many Military bands that performed in The Glen. The band HM Welsh Guards. The postcard posted in August 1923.

CHILDREN'S PLAYGROUND, CAROLINE'S GLEN, BRISTOL

80. In the 1950's Caroline's Cake Shops owned The Glen. A large play area for children, as depicted on this postcard. As well as famous Caroline's refreshments and teas.

81. Coldharbour Road (formerly Coldharbour Lane). The houses built c. 1904. This postcard published by Wilkinson of Trowbridge. Postally used in 1905.

82. Coldharbour Road in the opposite direction c. 1905. The turning on the left Devonshire Road. Further along on the right by the 3-story house and shop, Greendale Road.

83. St. Albans Road from Coldharbour Road, a winter scene, the bare trees affording good views of the terraced houses. At the far end the road joins with North View and Linden Road.

84. The horse and cart owned by Mr. W.H. Hughes, who ran an Off Licence, the Royal Oak, in Lower Redland Road.

85. Harcourt Road, showing a small selection of shops, near the corner with Coldharbour Road. The draper's shop showing a window tightly packed with goods for sale. c. 1905.

86. Further down Harcourt Road, large double bay houses with rooms in the roof. The field and trees in the distance bordering Redland Green, before the houses in Metford Road were built c. 1913.

87. Coldharbour Road at the crossroad with Linden Road, a road sign on the right. Today a traffic light junction. Looking straight ahead the houses in Halsbury Road. The open field beyond where Kellaway Avenue was developed.

88. Linden Road from North View, at the junction with Howard Road left, and almost opposite St. Albans Road. This view looking towards picture 87.

INDEX